Tracery

Tracery

THE ART OF SOUTHERN DESIGN

PAIGE SUMBLIN SCHNELL

written with ELEANOR LYNN NESMITH

STEWART, TABORI & CHANG

NEW YORK

Contents

My Story

 PEOPLE SOMETIMES ASK ME how I learned "design." I believe some of it is innate—we are all builders and creative problem solvers at heart—and the rest is learned. I learned design from architecture school, of course, but also from the world around me: my experiences, my family, my colleagues, and my home.

I fondly remember an early experience that changed me and started me down this path. When I was about eight years old, my parents asked if I would like to join them for an antiques auction in Glenwood, Alabama. Excited at the prospect, I didn't hesitate to join them. We walked through the building, looking at all of the available pieces and selecting those we would bid on. We finally selected a wardrobe for my room. It wasn't one of a kind—there were multiples of the same item from a hotel—but it was the right design for my needs and my room. The bidding started, and I held my breath. I was thrilled when we were the highest bidders. Amazingly, I still have that wardrobe. If you saw it in my home today, you probably wouldn't even notice it. It's a simple oak wardrobe, but it was the first piece of furniture I ever selected, and it represents an important moment for me. In retrospect, it was a powerful experience to see a piece of furniture not as an everyday object but one for which the design truly matters.

I grew up in the small town of Opp, Alabama, the daughter of a farmer and a teacher. We lived most of my childhood in a classic early 1900s home with wraparound porches, traditional cottage columns, and big oak trees in the front yard. It had a unique feel in the neighborhood as a once-solitary country house that was slowly enveloped by new, more

OPPOSITE ❋ In my heart, I guess I'll always be a country girl. Our family's contemporary farmhouse nods to the pioneering spirit of the past and looks to an optimistic future for living in harmony with the land.

contemporary development. Today, I carry with me that house and a love for old mixed with new. That house—and that idea—still resonates in my designs.

My two sisters, Megan and Maggie, and I played on the porches every day. Those porches were the perfect place to retreat from the summer sun in south Alabama. They were functional in other ways, too: We spent many days building things on those porches. Among other things, we built elaborate houses for our Barbie dolls out of found and repurposed objects. My mother Pam's simple premise—that we should be creative and build Barbie's dream house rather than buying it—was something that shifted my life's path. The first room I designed was for my Barbie doll. I can still see it in my mind.

I became a mother at a young age. My wonderful daughter, Mallory, and I left my hometown together to head to college. As one might imagine (or maybe know from firsthand experience), being a young mother was full of challenges, and I'm thankful for all who helped me along the way. But, as any parent knows, the experience can bring out the best in you. A young mother is nothing if not creative—by necessity—and I learned to be decisive, finish tasks quickly, and make the best of any situation.

Ultimately, I graduated with a degree in interior architecture from Auburn University. It wasn't a very direct path for me to the School of Architecture, but when I sat down for my first studio class, I knew I was home.

Mallory was a nearly constant companion in the architecture school studio. She knew most of my classmates and professors and was a vivacious little girl who would talk to anyone in the school. Sometimes people ask how I make so many decisions in a day while working on projects. I think it was my experiences as a single mom in a challenging and top-ranked architecture school that made the difference. An interior designer makes countless decisions every day—you need to be confident in each decision, and then be prepared to quickly move on to the next one. In a

sense, I think Mallory taught me that. Mallory is now in college—this time to get her own degree—and I like to say that this is actually her second time in college.

My time at Auburn had a huge impact on my understanding of design and its core elements, such as proportion and scale. It's where I learned to be confident in my designs, and where I first found my "voice" in design. I learned to go for it and push the limits, but always be sure the design is appropriate. That's the essence of Auburn's approach: Design is not about me, as the designer—it's about the end user. Those lessons that I learned at school are still what fundamentally guide me today. They are the foundation of my designs.

I had my first taste of professional life when one of my college professors designed a new farmhouse for my dad, Andy, and my stepmother, Anne. They gave me an opportunity to be involved in the interior design, and I loved watching that house go from dream to reality. It was a great experience to have a small role in it. This was my first real house design. I

The front porch of our Seagrove home is a favorite spot for Mark, Mallory, and me to relax.

spent the next few years designing exclusively commercial spaces before eventually making my way back to a practice that included residential design too.

After graduating from Auburn, I moved to the South's "big city"—Atlanta—to start my career as an interior designer. As I drove from Alabama into the city on Interstate 85 for the first night in our new home, Mallory slept in the backseat, and I listened to a book-on-tape by author and Southern commentator Rick Bragg. When the iconic skyline appeared straight ahead, his humorous observation about the city reverberated through the car and my head: "Atlanta is about as Southern as a snowmobile." I was scared. Even though Atlanta is only four hours from my hometown, it felt at that moment like another planet. It's hard to grow if you're never willing to leave your comfort zone. This was one of those times. Mallory and I started a new chapter.

My first job out of college was at the large multidisciplinary firm ASD, headquartered in downtown Atlanta. At ASD I learned not only design but how a project actually comes to fruition. I was inspired by my colleagues—their talent, dedication, and kindness. My years at ASD allowed me to grow and really find my place in the design world.

I met my husband, Mark, in Atlanta. There are people who change your life. He is that person for me. Like me (and countless others) he arrived in the city for a new job, and we met through friends in our respective offices. Mark is an urban designer, so he works on large-scale projects. Between the two of us, we cover a lot of ground in the design world, and yet there's a surprising amount of crossover. We influence each other's work, serve as our most trusted critics, and even collaborate on projects from time to time. I love coming home to someone who has the same passion as I do. We live, eat, and breathe design. Travel and dinner-party discussions are especially fun with a husband who is also a designer. Now our daughter, Mallory, is pursuing a creative career, as she works toward a degree in art and photography. I guess the apple truly

We love entertaining at home, and a round dining table is so congenial and best for conversation. Two leaves expand it to seat ten. Its rounded edges encourage easy flow, and that's important since it stands in the middle of the room. The heavy German hutch was originally dark and dated, so I painted it a bold shade of green for a more contemporary look.

doesn't fall far from the tree, but then again, I don't know how she could avoid it in a family like ours.

After three years of dating and living the urban Atlanta life, Mark and I moved to a small beach town along the Gulf of Mexico in northwest Florida and got married. We made a leap from the heart of the city to a cottage on a dirt road, at least initially. We now live just down the road from that cottage, in Seagrove Beach, one in the string of beautiful communities along Scenic Highway 30A. The first New Urbanist town, Seaside, is within walking distance of our home, and my shop is in another renowned New Urbanist town called Rosemary Beach.

Everything about this place exudes design. It's one of the world's most amazing laboratories for urban design, architecture, and interior design. A remarkable number of towns, buildings, and interiors along 30A are the vision of extremely talented designers, and many are featured on the pages of magazines and books. There is no lack of inspiration in the area, and living in this environment has taken my designs to the next level.

It's within this history and context that I operate my firm, Tracery. It has always focused first and foremost on design. The studio at Tracery is a creative environment where ideas thrive. I always believe that two heads are better than one in a creative endeavor, and that is how I run Tracery. I love bouncing ideas off others and taking design to the next level.

I am constantly designing. Whether sitting on the beach, cooking dinner for my family and friends, or hanging out with our dog, Lucy, I am always walking through projects in my head. I love design and creating homes that our clients adore. After all, that's the ultimate measure of success. In the end, I have created a home.

One of my favorite quotes from one of my favorite clients sums it up: "I wake up every morning and have to pinch myself to make sure that living in this home is real and not just a dream."

OPPOSITE ⚜ I don't think I'll ever tire of the view of the beach on the Gulf of Mexico or living along Scenic 30A.

Traces of Home

 FEW WORDS CONJURE UP more emotional responses than *home*. There is the fundamental element of shelter, and it's remarkable how much a building contributes to our emotional security. Ideally, home is where we feel grounded, where we are loved, where we can be ourselves. The early twentieth-century French philosopher Gaston Bachelard wrote in *Poetics of Space*, "If I were asked to name the chief benefit of the house, I should say: the house shelters day-dreaming, the house protects the dreamer, the house allows one to dream in peace." That's a lot of responsibility on someone whose mission is to design a place to live. You wouldn't trust just anybody to do it. Yet it's truly impressive how some designers have the ability to accomplish all that and more.

Major metropolitan areas like Chicago, New York, Atlanta, and San Francisco like to claim they are the center of design and fashion, but I would argue that our twenty-mile stretch of beach in northwest Florida, known simply as Scenic Highway 30A, might have more talented designers and artists per capita than anywhere else in America.

When I lived in Washington, DC, all my friends were lawyers or lobbyists. When I moved to Florida to work for the town of Seaside, an eighty-acre planned community that spawned an international movement that has come to be known as New Urbanism, nearly everybody I met was an architect, interior designer, photographer, or artist. (Okay, there are a few real estate agents and restaurateurs in the mix.)

Since my vocation is writing about architecture and interiors, it was incredibly convenient for networking, both personally and professionally.

One of the many talented folks I met, first in a social setting, was Paige Sumblin Schnell, owner of Tracery. Not long after our first meeting I was invited to her home for one of her famous impromptu dinner parties. Gatherings are held for no real reason or for momentous occasions, major holidays, or simply to celebrate the fact that her daddy just brought down some field peas and corn fresh from the farm.

Paige and her husband, Mark, a highly accomplished urban designer, live in a simple cracker-style cottage (see page 132). Despite its straight-forward appearance from the street, this is a house filled with surprises. A revolving mix of antiques, art, comfy upholstered furniture, and a large round dining table fill up the loft-like living room. Thanks to exposed structural elements, the feeling is fundamental rather than elaborate, with a strong sense of harmony, just like Paige.

I wasn't the only one taken by the charm of the cottage. A week earlier a national magazine editor had stopped in and wanted to publish the house, and I got the assignment. That article led to other magazine features on Paige and Tracery, as well as a budding friendship grounded in our shared interest in design, not to mention relaxing on the beach and swimming in the Gulf. It was actually while sitting on the beach last summer that we conjured up the idea for this book and that we would team up on the effort.

Although I adored Paige's own home, it was only after I had visited homes she had designed for clients that I realized the depth of her talent and range of her aesthetic. Since Tracery was established in 2003, Paige has amassed an impressive portfolio of gracious interiors that merge Southern charm with European sensibilities, alongside an appreciation for architectural scale and proportions; her work transcends a singular style and defies a label. Paige has built Tracery's reputation on a commitment to soulful designs with traditional, vernacular, and continental influences, while never sacrificing comfort and the owner's own personality.

From the beginning, Tracery was a boutique in Rosemary Beach, as well as a design studio. The shop's offerings of furniture, original art, lighting, accessories, and antiques are all arranged in artful displays reflecting the firm's talents for melding diverse styles. One corner might contain a play of aqua and coral throw pillows, while another room is full of soothing neutrals and layers of texture. Having a retail storefront along pedestrian-friendly Main Street in a fashionable resort community brought in a number of commissions in Rosemary Beach, as well as in other nearby waterfront communities. It wasn't unusual for a casual shopper to become Paige's next major project.

Four of the houses in this book are located within a few blocks of each other in Seagrove, the older beach town where both Paige and I live. The homes couldn't be more different in form or function. One is a bright, sunny beach house rising three floors, with panoramic views over the Gulf, while another is a full-time family home with equal measures of urbane elegance and down-home comfort for an up-and-coming fashion designer.

In addition to the work along the coast, Tracery landed several ambitious full-time residences in Birmingham. Another turning point came in 2009, when *Southern Living* magazine tapped Tracery to design its

LEFT ❀ The shop recently expanded and is constantly changing its inventory and adding new lines.

RIGHT ❀ Design is a collaborative effort at Tracery, and a spirit of professional and personal camaraderie is the management style. The studio conference table is equally fitting for staff meetings, employee birthday celebrations, and client presentations.

ABOVE ❈ A new keeping room creates a gracious transition between an historic Tudor home and a major addition.

OPPOSITE ❈ Marble countertops and backsplash provide the perfect balance of sophistication and function for an open kitchen in a Rosemary Beach vacation home.

Cinnamon Shore "Idea House" in Port Aransas, Texas. More recently, the firm's geographical reach is expanding, with work in North and South Carolina, Georgia, Oklahoma, Tennessee, and Colorado.

The range of projects keeps things interesting at the studio. Paige's versatility as a designer is such that she transitions easily from a cozy gulf-front cottage filled with pieces upholstered in a colorful waterproof fabric to a grand Tudor renovation animated with nineteenth-century antiques and silk without missing a beat.

The one constant is the fact that each home is a reflection of the individual owner's taste and style. Paige refuses to repeat the same design in house after house. She recounts how clients will come to her

because they have seen one of the Tracery houses, and they want that exact design. Rather than give them a copy, Paige insists on pushing them into exploring new avenues. Paige gets the clients to talk, and she listens. The result is a home tailored to their lifestyle.

Paige's entire body of work, as well as the nineteen projects on these pages, is a testament to her signature approach of eschewing any one style, which is not to say that she's not designing in a voice distinctly her own. Each and every project is executed with passion and personal attention to detail. Obediently following the precepts of scale and proportion while at times joyfully breaking the rules, Paige creates updated classics—but not in the conventional sense. She combines materials,

forms, textures, and colors to form highly personalized environments like an artist might create a three-dimensional collage.

Despite her single-minded vision, Paige relishes the process of collaboration. Ideas are investigated and discussed and expanded with architects and other design professionals and associates at the firm. Although Paige is completely hands-on in the design process from beginning to end, she quickly acknowledges the roles and contributions of her talented associates. Designer Anna Kay Porch joined Tracery in 2005 and works alongside Paige on the execution of most projects.

From mentoring interns to making friends with homeowners, Paige's enthusiasm for design is infectious. Right from the first client meeting, each project brings inspiration, collaboration, and personal connections. Paige relishes the thrill of travel as much as the joys of a day sitting on the beach in Seagrove, and she does both with passion and purpose. (And yes, sitting on the beach has a purpose.) Numerous interviews for this book were conducted under an umbrella overlooking the Gulf. The Aspen text was discussed on the chairlift the day after the photo shoot and finalized sitting by the stone fireplace.

Paige believes a home should be appropriate and responsive to its surroundings. Whether in a city, along the water, in the mountains, on a farm, or anywhere in between, these houses are a thoughtful reflection of a particular place, climate, and culture. Accordingly, Paige's creations invite participation of the mind and body, and the opportunity for multiple interpretations. But in the end, it's the clients who meld their own home through years of their visual and physical interaction within a framework of the structure. And that's the way it should be.

The homes on these pages are personal, thoughtful, and contented . . . setting the stage for life. They lay a foundation for good days, and foster lasting memories. Choosing a color palette, selecting furnishings, or solving a spatial arrangement are second nature to Paige. First and foremost, Paige has a gift for getting to the essence of the matter at hand.

OPPOSITE ❊ In this Nashville home, the architecture spells out gentle patterns, rhythms, and textures. Even in more formal spaces, I relax the mood and introduce surprises.

Enduring Style

A well-designed house is at ease with a mix of personal items and exquisite objects.

Timeless spaces are restrained, balanced, and don't succumb to the obvious.

Tudor Renaissance

THE NOTION OF the great American house has diverse origins and deep roots. The decades leading up to the 1920s were surely a hallmark of residential design in both grand and modest terms. Throughout the South, Greek Revival mansions, Mediterranean villas, French chateaux, Tudor houses, and English country manors sprang up in blossoming garden suburbs. Mountain Brook, Alabama, with its rolling hills, winding tree-lined streets, lush gardens, and pedestrian shopping villages, is a testament to this epoch of town planning and architecture.

For me, an ambitious renovation of a classic Tudor-style home on a wooded hillside property offered endless possibilities. I teamed up with Jeff Dungan of Dungan Nequette Architects for an addition that would nearly double the home's original size. Although construction of the original house started in the 1920s, the Depression hit before it was completed. All the character had been lavished on the exterior, while the interiors, with their mundane materials and lack of detail, seemed like an afterthought. And they had never been updated. It was a blank canvas inside the walls of a beautiful box.

First we added a grand foyer, stairway, and balcony in keeping with Tudor traditions. Floors throughout are reclaimed wood and terra-cotta. Walls are rich wood paneling, antiqued mirrors, and stone. We introduced

OPPOSITE ❀ Two contemporary paintings, French antiques, and a grandfather clock gracefully come together to create a sophisticated vignette in a corner of the formal living room.

focal points and long views through rooms, creating seamless transitions between old and new.

The house possesses a distinct formality, yet there's a welcoming sequence from room to room. The scale and proportion of the new kitchen and keeping room are now remarkably similar to the obviously more proper living and dining rooms, conferring importance to everyday family spaces.

Although the house is majestic in its architectural expression, it succeeds in welcoming, not overwhelming. And now, nearly a century after construction started on this house, it is finally coming into its own. Enveloped in a lush garden of native oak-leaf hydrangeas, seasonal blooming flowers, and mature trees, this rambling structure is impossible to view in one glance. It's truly a country home in the city—and proof that patience is a virtue.

A grand double-height foyer now welcomes visitors. Substantial archways establish a hierarchy between the home's more formal rooms and family spaces. Art and books fill the paneled bookcases of the library wrapping around the balcony.

In the living room, interior refinements convey a sense of order and graciousness, while the historic framework offers an opportunity to introduce contemporary comfort.

OPPOSITE ABOVE ✿ The original rear servants' hall was opened up to create the niche in the dining room. People live differently today even in a grand home.

OPPOSITE BELOW ✿ Floor-to-ceiling metal windows, exposed beams, a steeply sloping ceiling, and a massive stone fireplace characterize the keeping room and create an engaging transition between old and new.

LEFT ✿ A marble bowl and antique table enliven a powder room located off the foyer discreetly tucked under the stairway.

OVERLEAF ✿ Recessed antique mirrored glass walls flank a large, light-filled niche in the dining hall. A mirror-on-mirror defines one recess, while an ornate framed painting on the opposite wall interrupts the symmetry of the space.

OPPOSITE ❊ The kitchen's relaxed elegance radiates with a tapestry of natural materials and textured finishes. Painted and stained cabinets combine with butcher-block and stone counters to break up the scale of the space.

LEFT ❊ This corner cabinet was the first piece we bought. It occupies a prominent spot adjoining the kitchen and keeping room. Its patina sets the tone for kitchen and inspired the overall color palette. Collected art reflects the family's varied interests.

RIGHT ❋ A master suite should be a refuge. An antique upholstered bench enlivens an inviting hallway between public spaces and the owners' private retreat.

OPPOSITE ❋ Plush fabrics and darker tones are embracing. The bed nestles into an upholstered niche. There is something comforting in sleeping in a cozy space that cradles you.

White marble floors and counters and a deep soaking tub instill timeless appeal in the master bath. The antique dressing mirror echoes the deep green walls of the bedroom.

RIGHT ❈ Upstairs, a procession of rooms creates an inviting flow through the house with the studio as a focal point at the terminus to draw one down the long hallway.

OPPOSITE ABOVE ❈ The light and airy studio is located above the new porte cochere and connects the main house with a new attached guesthouse.

OPPOSITE BELOW ❈ Exterior materials were carefully selected and crafted to create a seamless transition between the original house and the new construction.

ABOVE ❀ A pair of asymmetrical gables and a low stone wall announce the front of the house, creating a welcoming formal entry.

BELOW ❀ A sheltered porch nestled along the side of the house establishes an inviting approach for family and friends using the back door.

OPPOSITE ❀ The balance between the formal architecture and the informality of nature is a large measure of this home's appeal. Garden sculptures and a sink crafted from antique millstones enliven an intimate courtyard tucked amid the lush landscape.

Lofty Lakeside Living

LAKE MARTIN is a special place for anyone who grew up in Alabama. When it was created in 1926 with the damming of the Tallapoosa River, it was the largest man-made body of water in the world. Although it has lost that ranking, it's still the biggest lake in Alabama and enjoys a distinctive tradition of lakeside architecture, from the mysterious Russell cabins along the bluffs built for the company's textile workers in the 1930s to elegant new homes by some of the South's leading designers.

A couple from Birmingham was starting construction of a weekend home when I came to this project. The site was a stunning peninsula in a desirable neighborhood known as The Ridge, but the original plans were incomplete. With such a setting comes an inherent expectation of quality and a mandate to defer to nature. It was an incredible location and a chance for me to guide both the architecture and interior décor. At the time, it was an ambitious commission for a firm less than five years old. Today, it's still one of my favorite projects.

OPPOSITE ✷ A French sofa table crafted of reclaimed wood stands between identical sofas with tall arching backs. Furniture is placed for flexibility and multiple conversation areas. Modern Windsor-style chairs crafted of aluminum encircle a wood table with primitive lines, which doubles as a breakfast nook and a spot for games on rainy days.

The clients had only a few requests: utterly inviting, comfortable for a family with four young children, and most important, all white. Working with my associate, Anna Kay Porch, we responded with planked wooden walls swathed throughout in Benjamin Moore's China white. A single paint color is an incredibly easy and effective way to instill continuity. Against that monochromatic background we layered rough-hewn beams and pillars of reclaimed barn wood from New England and Georgia. Underfoot are antique oak floors, hand-stained with a textured finish, and a mix of sea-grass and fine antique rugs.

Although the traditional lake house is casual with a loose organization of spaces, this structure is far from a modest cottage. The home's grand hall rises to thirty-five feet with floor-to-ceiling windows looking out to the water. The vigor of the materials and the scale of the room called for furnishings of equal bearing. Modern touches with their own sculptural quality, upholstered pieces in linen and cotton, and galvanized accessories counter a few softly stated French antiques and an antique Italian chandelier. These pleasing contrasts create vitality and make the spaces come alive.

So much family life centers around the kitchen, and this space is open and always ready for action. Paired marble-topped islands offer a designated prep area and one for casual dining.

Neither the architecture nor furnishings are confined to a single style or period, making this home sometimes hard to describe and impossible to label. To me, it's simply a classic lake house where family and friends get away—and relaxation is always on the itinerary.

Two rugged fieldstone pillars and massive posts and beams lend an air of permanence to the dining room. A custom-designed pedestal table of antique oak accommodates large gatherings and entertaining. A nineteenth-century Italian chandelier hangs from the second-floor balcony. Contemporary seats slipcovered in white linen combine with antique Italian armchairs updated with faux leather and a soft floral print.

The art of cooking is social and visually exciting, especially at a weekend home. A pair of four-foot-square islands with dark-stained maple legs and honed Carrera marble sets the perimeter of the kitchen. Bongo stools with nail-head trim surround one, while the other accommodates a microwave and warming drawers.

RIGHT ❀ Six-inch-wide pine planks with a quarter-inch spacing create the feel of an old lake cottage. There's not an inch of Sheetrock in the entire house. The wood walls and cabinets are painted Benjamin Moore China white throughout. Open shelving with jigsaw brackets display vintage white stoneware.

OPPOSITE ❀ We took full advantage of the pantry's twelve-foot-high ceilings. A rolling library ladder accesses upper cabinets. Shelves with glass-fronted sliding doors are sleek and practical. Along the bottom, two dishwashers provide for cleanup out of view.

OPPOSITE ❈ Tall windows flood this sophisticated guest suite with natural daylight. Neutrals are enlivened with two French antique armchairs and a headboard upholstered with soft linen paisley. Dressmaker details and shiny white buttons add special touches to simple linen draperies.

LEFT ❈ The adjoining guest bath is a luxurious retreat from top to bottom. The floor is Carrera marble tiles in a herringbone pattern and the ceiling is wood-plank paneling. A long porcelain tub takes in uninterrupted views down to the lake. The fabric and detailing of the curtains are the same as in the bedroom.

ABOVE ❈ The house is predominantly white but we added flourishes of color in the children's bedrooms. Contemporary metal canopy beds and industrial-style drapery hardware enliven the boys' bedroom. Pillows with a bold geometric pattern and a striped, blue-and-white wool rug are kid-friendly.

BELOW ❈ Pink damask draperies and a comfy chaise lounge add feminine touches to the daughter's room. A hint of pink says girl, but it's sophisticated enough for guests.

OPPOSITE ❈ Black-and-white family photographs line the stairway wall. A graceful silhouette defines the railing and an antique painted chest creates a focal point at the landing.

OPPOSITE ❈ An upholstered headboard in the master was custom designed in proportion with the room's high ceilings. Silk pillows in gray and aqua dress up the neutral palette, and a large crystal chandelier and mirrored side table enhance the luxurious spirit.

LEFT ❈ The juxtaposition of rustic charm and urbane style continues in the master bath. Contemporary sinks rest within a massive custom vanity crafted of reclaimed wood with soft curves and rounded edges. Ornate wall sconces are mounted next to large-scale mirrors.

RIGHT ❧ A more casual seating area is located behind the double fireplace. A sectional sofa nestles against the window wall, and sheer linen draperies soften the sturdy simplicity of the post-and-beam carpentry.

OPPOSITE ❧ The house sits on a prominent site, taking in panoramic views of Lake Martin.

Steeped in Tradition

A HISTORIC HOME deserves respect, and I take pleasure in creating interiors in keeping with the original architecture. When previous clients purchased a 1926 Mediterranean Revival-style house, I relished the chance to work with them again, this time enhancing a landmark structure, designed by Martin-Hosmer Studios, one of Florida's leading firms of the period. Our goal was to come up with a fresh approach in keeping with the family's decidedly more relaxed lifestyle while writing the next chapter of the home's storied history.

Additions and modifications had been made over the decades, yet the original bones and unique features were firmly intact. The house possessed a carved limestone fireplace, ornate Venetian columns, and elegant wood and stone floors with tile inlays. Although the house is grand in its aspirations, the original layout of rooms enjoys a surprisingly intimate scale and romantic proportions.

The dark wood finish of the original floors, numerous French doors, and tall windows prompted us to lighten the walls. Anna Kay Porch and I had worked with the owners on their prior house just across the street, so we already had a solid understanding of their desires and requirements. We chose subtle neutral tones on the walls to accentuate the architectural details, including a series of recessed niches perfect for showcasing an impressive art collection.

OPPOSITE ❁ Furniture placement accentuates original architectural details. A painting by Barbara Krupp resides in a niche in the living room. The vibrant oranges and reds spin off the canvas and flow throughout.

One of the most appealing aspects of the home is its openness and the way rooms flow into one another, with exuberant archways and architectural embellishments that enhance the sense of procession. I wove a bold palette of reds and greens throughout the house in the furnishings and accessories. This wave of color was inspired in part by a favorite painting that is prominently displayed in the living room. We embraced the idea of a red dining room, but turned it on its head, opting for light walls with all the color coming from upholstery, rugs, and window treatments in various textures and vermillion shades.

Working with clients on the preservation of an architectural jewel reflective of its time and place was a privilege. The restored home now proudly stands along the water as a testament to their commitment.

OPPOSITE ❈ Ornate columns supporting an archway create a lively interchange between the formal living and dining rooms of this historic home. A consistent and complementary color palette enhances the procession between spaces.

ABOVE ❈ Works by Mitchell Lonas are artfully displayed in a second niche in the living room.

ABOVE ❈ The generous dimensions of the original rooms allowed for a sitting area in this guest bedroom. Bold patterned draperies hanging from ceiling to floor create drama in a room of any size.

OPPOSITE ❈ Layers of textures, materials, and colors instill the breakfast room with character. Classic terra-cotta, clay tiles, and a pecky cypress inlaid on the ceiling add character, while colorful patterned and striped fabrics introduce contemporary touches.

Fashion
Starts at Home

NOT ALL HOUSES at the beach are "beach houses." Although most people who make a conscious decision to live full-time along the water appreciate the inherent casual lifestyle, that doesn't mean high style needs to be compromised. That's especially true for Stephanie Carter, the founder of Southern Fashion House.

When Stephanie set up her first retail shop in Florida ten years ago, she was content living in a dated 1980s beach house a block from the Gulf of Mexico in Seagrove, Florida. As her fashion empire grew to include three signature brands, she realized she needed a home that reflected her lifestyle. I was already a customer of Deja Vu, her shop in Seaside, when we were introduced by mutual friends. It turns out we grew up forty miles apart in rural Alabama. We already respected each other's talents and hit it off immediately on a personal level.

Surrounded by pattern and color in her fast-paced career, Stephanie prefers to dial down the volume a bit at the end of the day. Because a fashion designer must be constantly changing with every season, we created a house with good bones and the option to mix it up on a whim. The backdrop is intentionally muted and monochromatic, allowing Stephanie to experiment with fabrics, patterns, and colors according to the seasons. The multi-shades-of-gray palette provides the perfect stage for layering and pairing of textures and materials.

OPPOSITE ❈ One central space is not actually a room, but a closet, a capacious sanctuary carved out of the former loft. A testament to fashion, shelves accommodate Manolo Blahnik heels, Tony Lama cowboy boots, vintage Louis Vuitton luggage, and Stephanie's own Southern Fashion House collections.

ABOVE ❈ The master suite mingles industrial with elegant. A plush upholstered headboard and sweeping curtains of raw silk in gray and eggplant pair with a canopy crafted of galvanized water pipes. A rolling screen crafted of antique doors adds charm and elusive transparency between the bedroom and bath.

OPPOSITE ❈ The dressing area repeats unexpected pairings. An arch and mirrored walls define the space with an antique dressing table rounding out the ensemble. Deer antlers bow to Stephanie's rural Alabama roots and display jewelry sold at her retail shops.

We raised the roof to add clerestory windows for light, creating a dramatic ceiling in the living room. Pecky cypress paneling and beams introduce volume and warmth. The added height accommodates Stephanie's cherished antique doors that now rest above the mantel and a commanding chandelier that we relocated from one of her retail shops. A new archway enhances the home's grander scale in keeping with the chandelier, fireplace, and antique sideboard and mirror. The dining room table was another prior possession, which we paired with an upholstered bench and slipcovered chairs compatible with casual family meals and informal entertaining.

Like Stephanie's approach to fashion, the house sways from exquisite élan to kid-friendly comfort without missing a beat. For all the unbridled urbanity, it's first and foremost a year-round family home that's a perfect retreat to kick up your heels or kick off your shoes and just relax.

ABOVE ❋ Like Stephanie's fashion approach, a lively interplay of sophistication and casual comfort inform the interior décor. A lower ceiling height and an upholstered bench create an intimate space for the dining table.

RIGHT ❋ The foyer's new archway frames the living room and accentuates the raised ceiling clad in pecky cypress. The added height allows for clerestory windows, a pair of antique doors above the fireplace, and a large chandelier.

OPPOSITE ❋ Stephanie's antique sideboard and tall mirror are more suited to the home's new, grander scale, while a slipcovered linen sofa, jute rug, and cowhide ottoman add down-to-earth comfort.

Spirit of Place

The most beloved homes are respectful of their surroundings

and a reflection of their owners.

Altitude Adjustment

CERTAIN MOUNTAIN HOUSES, by their very elevation, heighten the pleasures of a ski vacation or cool getaway in summer. Set along the ridge overlooking Aspen Highlands and Maroon Bells, this Colorado house is perfectly tailored for large family gatherings and holidays.

I was just finishing the clients' permanent residence when they purchased a mountain retreat, a recently completed home boasting classic Aspen-style architecture, large acreage, and panoramic views.

Crafted of native farmer's stone, the house is large but nestled discreetly amid spruce, firs, and of course, aspens. So discreetly, in fact, it would be easy to miss if not for the white twinkle lights wrapping half a dozen trees along the road. But once you turn into the winding drive, the charm of the property starts to unfold. Even before you enter the house, the expansive glass front door allows a peek through the living room to the mountains beyond.

My clients had been coming to Aspen for years, so they had an understanding and appreciation of a Western aesthetic. I believe that embracing an owner's style makes all the difference in creating a truly personal home. They wanted warm fabrics, deep colors, aged leathers, and textured finishes.

The stone of the exterior is repeated in the four interior fireplaces, setting the stage for earth tones throughout. The peaked ceiling rises to

OPPOSITE ❈ Completely open to long views over the expansive landscape and mountains beyond, the stone terrace accommodates a generous dining table and sitting area. Even on winter days the southern exposure creates a sunny setting for entertaining or simply relaxing.

thirty feet in the living room, so the scale of the furniture must be in keeping with the scale of the space. I chose two facing sofas, deep and luxurious for lounging, along the window wall rather than several pairs of chairs. A custom-designed leather daybed is placed on axis with the front door to define two more-intimate areas without restricting long views out.

Because three families share the home, I created three master suites, each with its own personality, furnishings, and finishes. Always in my thoughts were the stunning vistas as I placed the furniture in the bedrooms.

It's surprising how designing a house in Aspen is so similar to a home along the Gulf of Mexico. The background is white sandy beaches and emerald waters or snowcapped mountains and bright blue skies. Both places are all about the views and connecting with the great outdoors.

OPPOSITE ⟡ I love to play on the idea of taking refuge in the pastoral landscape of the mountains. The view outside this second-floor guest suite sets a soothing tone.

ABOVE ⟡ As soon as I walked through the front door, I realized the scale of the living room called for layering and depth. Plush upholstered sofas and a pair of leather armchairs fill the space, while a medley of wool and velvet pillows and throws add warmth and texture.

ABOVE ❀ A neutral palette with accents of texture and subtle pattern sets the tone for all the bedrooms. The constantly changing landscape outside the window of this first-floor master suite adds all the necessary color to the composition.

BELOW ❀ A trio of double beds set end-to-end and tucked under the eaves accommodates family and friends. The generous loft-style space features corner play areas.

OPPOSITE ❀ A massive stone fireplace and a series of framed archways characterize this sheltered terrace. Comfortable furniture and a rug enhance the feel of a year-round outdoor room.

Small-Town Values

ONE OF THE THINGS I love about my practice is the variety of work. I enjoy working closely with homeowners who are intimately involved with every detail of the design of their home, but I also relish projects that by their very nature allow for artistic license, encourage experimentation, and offer a platform to showcase the depth of our firm's work.

Each year *Southern Living* magazine builds and features on their pages what they call an "Idea House." In 2009, the magazine tapped Tracery to design their Idea House in Texas.

After a terrific inaugural partnership, *Southern Living* came back to us three years later for a project in Georgia with the architecture firm Historical Concepts. It was the first time *Southern Living* had highlighted a renovation rather than new construction. The location was Senoia, a picture-perfect town brimming with old-fashioned Southern charm, which had been the setting for numerous movies such as *Driving Miss Daisy* and *Fried Green Tomatoes*. The town is the backdrop for the AMC television show *The Walking Dead*.

As part of the project, the structure was relocated to a ten-acre residential infill neighborhood developed by Scott Tigchelaar and adjacent to the historic downtown. Built in the 1830s, the house had witnessed additions and renovations that compromised some of its character. I

ABOVE ❂ The upholstered bed with a tufted headboard and footboard anchors the large master bedroom. Orange-striped linen accents and a skirted table with tailored box pleats introduce pattern and color.

OPPOSITE ❂ A wide central hallway runs the length of the home. Burlap draperies frame the front door and accentuate the sidelights, affording the foyer casual sophistication.

started with the concept of a hypothetical family who would move in and come to love this old house as their own. Whenever possible we salvaged materials and highlighted historical details. The original hand-planed wood paneling of the master bedroom was intact, so we featured it in our design.

A new wraparound porch was outfitted with a seating area and vintage farm table with benches facing the street. A dogtrot-style entry hallway runs through the house, establishing a welcoming and unpretentious first impression.

Walls were removed and spaces rearranged to carve out a new kitchen that flows into one large living space. Although the layout is contemporary in its openness, the overriding scale is intimate, proportions are familiar, and new rooms feel as if they evolved over time. A mix of antiques, vintage pieces, and comfortable new upholstered furnishings suggests the spirit of a collected home.

The town of Senoia lives in the past, present, and future through all the movies filmed there. I like to think our design respects the history of a simple farmhouse and sets the stage for a family to move in and write the next chapter.

ABOVE ❈ The large island sets off the kitchen in this open floor plan. The clean lines of the Shaker-style cabinets complement the detailing and materials of the original farmhouse.

BELOW ❈ Tucked in a sunny alcove, the dining room offers a casual twist on tradition as two wing chairs, a curved back settee, and a pair of rustic burlap-covered benches surround the table.

OPPOSITE ❈ A vintage console table set behind the sofa anchors the living room. A medley of framed and unframed art and vintage accessories rests on the mantel.

RIGHT ❀ Four chairs create an inviting conversation area on the side porch and take advantage of French doors opening into the dining room. The ceiling's classic baby blue hue is repeated in the accent pillows and rug.

OPPOSITE ❀ A new, deep porch wraps around the original farmhouse, creating a welcoming presence on the street corner.

Sheltered Existence

SOME BEACH HOUSES have their toes in the sand and head in the sunshine. Others happily reside in a shaded version of summer. The town of Seagrove, where Mark and I live, boasts a beautiful stretch of white sand and emerald waters. Seagrove is equally known for its gravel lanes that twist and turn amid old-growth trees. A house nestled within a sheltering canopy of live oaks and magnolia on one such street, and less than a block from the Gulf of Mexico, captured the attention of my clients. They were willing to overlook the structure's shortage of architectural charm and surplus of somber finishes.

A complete overhaul of the décor of a five-bedroom house is no small undertaking, but the metamorphosis was complete just in time for the summer season. Before the renovation, the tone felt like a city house, not at all appropriate for the coastal setting. One of the main goals when we design a second home is to make a break from the routine.

Time spent at the beach should be about sunshine, camaraderie, and leisure. Now a soothing seaside palette of blues, grays, and sandy hues sets a relaxing tone. Oak floors with a lime whitewash offer a lighter look that's appropriately casual, utterly sophisticated, and very forgiving of sandy feet.

In the kitchen, I replaced an imposing peninsula with two parallel islands, one for prep work and one for casual entertaining. Next

OPPOSITE ❈ The tall windows needed draperies, but the relatively small niche called for restraint. The fabric and panel curtains are a Tracery custom line.

ABOVE ⊗ The large kitchen accommodates two islands. The parallel configuration creates an efficient galley for cooking and separate space for counter dining.

OPPOSITE ⊗ Marble countertops, subway tile rising to the ceiling, and open shelves offer an attractive background for the open layout.

we removed the cherry cabinets and yellow granite countertops in the kitchen and pulled up dark carpeting in the bedrooms. A completely separate formal dining room was turned into a cozy den. The dining table now resides in a sunny alcove, creating a decidedly more friendly open living area. Low benches add a casual touch and are flexible when kids need to squeeze in. Two facing sofas maximize seating for family gatherings and encourage a gracious interchange between the living area and kitchen.

Taken as a whole, the home's soothing palette of cool coastal colors suggests a lazy, laid-back frame of mind. And that's an appealing proposition no matter the season or reason for coming to the beach.

Facing sofas call for an oversize table in keeping with the scale of a fireplace. The table is a custom design crafted from reclaimed wood. The garden stools echo the coastal blues of the landscape painting by local artist Sherry Sandquist.

Bedrooms in a beach house frequently are requested to do double duty. The teenage daughter's favorite colors were yellow and gray, so we used them in a sophisticated way to create a space equally inviting for guests. Three primary fabrics feature bold geometrical patterns for a contemporary edge. Bed linens are white washable fabrics for a crisp feel that's easy to maintain.

Located on the third level, a master retreat echoes themes of seaside relaxation and coastal refinement. French doors open onto a private porch nestled high amid the live oaks.

Sweet Home Alabama

I'VE LIVED AT THE BEACH for more than ten years, but in my heart I'll always be a farmer's daughter.

The land in south Alabama where I was raised is fertile, and my family has been growing cotton, corn, and peanuts there for generations. My father still works the land of his father and grandfather and great-grandfather, as well as additional acreage he has purchased, including a large spread along the Pea River.

When I was in architecture school at Auburn University, Daddy and my stepmother, Anne, built a house on the property. He had recently married Anne, who was an attorney in Birmingham with a thriving practice. We laughed that it was a 1990s version of *Green Acres* but with Anne as the professional from the city. Daddy was confident that a classic farmhouse on a bluff overlooking the flood plain of the river would make country living a lot more enticing.

I recommended one of my professors, Gaines Blackwell, to design the house, and I got my first real hands-on experience. He and I walked the property and drove the stakes for the foundation. Because I knew Daddy and Anne so well, I was able to translate their desires in terms of the look, layout, and function. I sat with Professor Blackwell at Auburn as he drew the plans.

Rather than rely on the more fanciful notions of Southern architecture, we tapped the region's utilitarian, agrarian roots for inspiration. A

ABOVE ❀ Engaging scale and traditional proportions forge familiar images of home. I like to think the structure has a rural vocabulary, spoken with a sophisticated Southern accent.

OPPOSITE ❀ The screen porch off the back of the house is a year-round entertaining space large enough to accommodate a gracious conversation area and a dining table for eight. Collected items and a vintage chest painted white enhance the feel of a well-appointed outdoor room.

sense of restraint is the architectural order. Familiar forms translate to deep wraparound porches and wide overhangs. Materials are straightforward and honest—board-and-batten siding and a steeply pitched metal roof.

Inside, the arrangement of rooms flows one to another with a sense of inevitability. The heart of the house is a serious cook's kitchen with a large island for casual meals. (There's not a lot of going out to eat in this part of Alabama.) The double-height living room and formal dining room strike just the right balance between rustic and refined, and acknowledge Anne's urbane sense of style that has yet to waver.

From the outset, the farmhouse was intended to be a family gathering place. Anne has five siblings, I have two sisters, and there are six grandchildren. A big crowd always comes for holidays, so the guest house comes in very handy. Recently Mark designed an outbuilding for boat storage and Anne's gardening projects. As with any true working farm, change is a constant. Next on the horizon is a big shed of a building that will house tractors by day and double as a party barn at night. Invitations will be highly coveted.

OPPOSITE ❈ The double-height ceiling lends an air of grandeur without pretense in this decidedly rural home. Furnishings and finishes are devoted to comfort and practicality.

ABOVE ❈ The kitchen's galley arrangement with casual dining along the island is an utterly functional layout. French doors offer easy access to dining on the screen porch, where homegrown vegetables are often on the menu.

The master suite reflects family. A medley of still-life paintings, landscapes, regional folk art, and photographs lines the walls. Furniture is a mix of antiques and cherished family pieces. A vase is filled with Indian hawthorn, which grows profusely on the property. The large silver peanut nods to the farm's leading cash crop.

RIGHT ❁ Although relatively modest in its dimensions and humble in its materials, the farmhouse is proud and worldly. Simple timber pillars and exposed rafters, rather than elaborate columns or embellishments, frame views from the porch of the expansive working farm.

OPPOSITE ❁ Farmers have long built in appropriate ways. Their structures for shelter and utility have a tradition of simple beauty and clean lines. A steeply pitched pyramidal roof crowns the guesthouse.

Crafted with Care

The most beautiful materials improve with time.

Evocative spaces are enduring in their appeal.

Good Neighbors

PEOPLE OFTEN ASK how clients come to hire our firm. Sometimes it starts with a friendly hello in the elevator.

Several years ago, a couple from Texas purchased property in Rosemary Beach and was renting an apartment in the same building as our studio. After a few chance encounters and more visits to our shop on Main Street, a block from their lot, the casual greetings turned into a commission. They had already hired Atlanta architect Peter Block. His scheme was a fresh take on the Dutch colonial architecture of Cape Town, South Africa, perfect for the cohesive streetscape and coastal setting. Flemish gables, tall windows, and a smooth white stucco exterior offer a seamless match for the sculptural arrangement of light-filled interiors.

With such a simple and elegant foundation, a crisp white palette enlivened with sensuous textures and natural materials was practically a given. The heart of the home is a grand central space where congregating, relaxing, cooking, and eating clearly signal a spirit of approachable elegance. A dining table resides on axis with the front door, and a tall window with soft flowing draperies offers a glimpse to a private landscaped courtyard. Floors are wide plank with a rough limed finish, and the soaring thirteen-foot-high ceilings are clad in whitewashed pecky cypress.

One of my favorite spaces is the cozy nook off the main living area. We repeated the pecky cypress on the walls. The plush linen sectional

OPPOSITE ❈ The house has such subtle architectural nuance, bold colors would have been overwhelming. Sometimes I use black as an accent tone. The iron T-back counter stools and the chalkboard train schedule artwork are all that is needed for contrast.

sofa practically fills up the whole room. Deliberately overscaled furniture can sometimes make a small space feel larger.

The best houses have a way of making people feel welcome and comfortable. Well-proportioned rooms awash with light from dusk to dawn enhance the hum of activity and the tranquility of a beach setting.

OPPOSITE ❈ Quiet but layered with detail, the living room relies on textures and silhouettes. The mirrored armoire stands as a counterpoint to the kitchen. The shell chandelier references the coastal setting.

LEFT ❈ Bathed in natural light, a ship-shaped curving stairway ascends to the loft-like third floor.

ABOVE ❈ Elegance and informality blend seamlessly in the dining room with a contemporary trestle table crafted of reclaimed wood. Sculptural wingback chairs with nail-head detailing round out the ensemble.

RIGHT ❈ A house is more inviting if you can stand in one room and see into the next. Overscaled furniture and fourteen-foot-high ceilings allow this cozy nook to hold its own as a convivial gathering spot.

OPPOSITE ABOVE ❈ A cheerful guestroom makes the most of the gabled roofline. The bed tucks nicely under the windows. Distressed metal pendant shades add weight to the lofty space.

OPPOSITE BELOW ❈ The house sits on a prominent corner lot practically next door to our shop in Rosemary Beach. Traditional forms, graceful balconies and timeless proportions establish a connection to community, utterly appropriate to life along the Gulf.

The Spice of Life

 EVERY STRETCH of the coast along the Gulf of Mexico has its own appeal. And every beach community has its own character. Cinnamon Shore, Texas, is more than eight hundred miles from Seagrove, where I live, yet in many ways it's closer to home than a lot of my projects.

First, my husband, Mark, is the urban designer of Cinnamon Shore. Mark's association started years earlier, when Jeff Lamkin was in the early stages of developing the Texas property near Port Aransas. He visited Scenic 30A and its famous New Urbanist communities to get ideas for his beach town. A mutual friend made an introduction, and soon Mark was hired to design the town plan and create the design code and color palette. As things were taking off in Cinnamon Shore, they landed the 2009 *Southern Living* Idea House.

In an early conceptual meeting, someone with *Southern Living* said they were hoping to use Dungan Nequette Architects and Tracery. Mark told me he literally laughed out loud and asked if they knew that Paige, the owner of Tracery, was his wife.

Obviously, everyone was in agreement that it was the perfect team. Architects Jeff Dungan and Louis Nequette and I work together regularly, so the design process moved along quickly, which is a necessity when working on these types of projects.

The house was laid out to accommodate multiple families who come together to the beach for vacations and holidays. The overriding spirit is fun. Although I've done my fair share of houses in which I reference muted tones from nature, this time I happily acknowledge everything

OPPOSITE LEFT ❁ Visiting friends and cousins are part of life's routine at a beach house. Railroad cars inspired the trio of built-in bunks that make the most of limited space in the loft.

OPPOSITE RIGHT ❁ A sunny alcove accommodates a picnic-style table, two slipcovered end chairs, and a built-in bench for casual coastal dining.

from vibrant beach umbrellas along the Mediterranean Sea to inflatable fluorescent beach balls to yellow polka-dot bikinis. Don't be afraid of color. I tell people it's like the first swim of the season: Just jump in. You are always glad you did.

Each of the two master suites has its own distinctive personality in terms of architecture and décor. The rolling barn door in an unforgettable shade of yellow and exuberant fabrics and black accents enliven one of the masters. The other boasts a bright orange stencil pattern on the walls and bed linens with an equally bold geometric pattern.

The house was open to tours throughout a summer and proved to be very popular. It also set a high-water mark for the town's future architecture, as well as its lifestyle. For me the most rewarding aspect was the fact that a couple bought the house as is. It's been more than five years, and they are living the dream we envisioned for our "family" with every trip to the beach.

OPPOSITE ❋ Balance beauty and utility in a kitchen. I chose Calcutta marble for the island and maple butcher-block counters for either side of the stove. A combination of crisp white and espresso cabinets enlivens the mix.

ABOVE ❋ The family room extends the length of the house, taking advantage of Gulf views. A slipcovered sofa creates a subtle distinction between the main sitting area and a casual grouping of four club chairs around an ottoman.

OPPOSITE ❈ Multiple master suites work well at a second home where there are often two families vacationing together. A glass wall separates the bath and bedroom for a sense of openness, while curtain panels can be closed for privacy.

ABOVE ❈ A graphic floral stencil pattern adorns the walls of the adjoining master bedroom.

BELOW ❈ A canary-yellow, sliding barn door mounted with galvanized hardware animates the upstairs master, echoing the Southern vernacular detailing of the exterior. Bed linens repeat the cheerful yellow and deeper gray tones of the bathroom walls.

Alys Beach Escape

THE CASUAL PLEASURES and ageless allure of the beach endure. Whether for a weekend or lifetime, it's impossible to resist the pull of the gracious homes and timeless architecture as well as the easy-come, easy-go attitude of the stretch of the Florida Panhandle known fondly as Scenic 30A.

Although there are no set rules on how to decorate a house in a coastal resort, I strive to find the perfect balance between casual and sophisticated, especially when outfitting a vacation rental home in the chic New Urbanist town of Alys Beach. There's an underlying elegance and confidence in the architectural aspirations of every structure in Alys Beach. The grandest civic structures, private homes, and the smallest details are all designed and executed with the same thought.

My good friend and talented architect Eric Watson, with whom Tracery has teamed up on other projects, designed this house with two symmetrical courtyards anchored by covered porches. The formal entry opens onto a sheltered porch and an inviting outdoor seating area, introducing a glimpse of good things to come.

Ever mindful of the architecture, we chose an exuberant color palette of corals and blues, starting in the courtyard and weaving throughout the house. The configuration also sets up interiors with a flowing arrange-

OPPOSITE ✣ Celebrate a sense of arrival. A louvered front gate beckons visitors into a covered porch and adjoining open courtyard. Elaborate Gothic arches covered with flowering vines add pattern and texture.

ment of rooms flooded with natural light. Bluestone flooring and white plaster walls further blur the lines between indoors and out.

A red cedar timber vaulted ceiling, rising to nearly eighteen feet high in the dining room, anchors the heart of the home. To soften the space and introduce color, I used tall curtains along both window walls. In the living area, upholstered pieces mix with linens and cottons chosen for comfort, appearance, and durability—a prerequisite for a vacation home. Art, accessories, and pillows add welcome accents of color.

Finding the right mix of fun and elegance is so important in a beach house. The question is how to make something beautiful without being too precious. This colorful getaway strikes the right chord and offers a lively backdrop for unforgettable days along the Gulf of Mexico.

ABOVE ❈ The design aesthetic of Alys Beach is predominantly white-washed masonry. To introduce a more relaxed coastal vibe, we paired natural wood surfaces with accents of coral and turquoise throughout.

OPPOSITE ❈ The stairway introduces a dramatic architectural element. The flooring changes from blue stone to dark wood to mark a transition from public to private spaces.

High ceilings, textured natural surfaces, and flowing spaces lend a
sense of grandeur without pretense.
A trio of abstract paintings by artist
Sherry Sandquist anchors the living
room's conversation area.

OPPOSITE ❈ The dining room is a sunny connector between the kitchen and living room. Five simple curtains frame views and echo the coral colors of the courtyard.

ABOVE ❈ Each bedroom is treated as a separate guest suite in this sophisticated vacation home.

BELOW LEFT ❈ In a guest suite with French doors opening onto the courtyard, a jute rug softens the stone floor and complements the contemporary sleigh bed crafted of reclaimed wood.

BELOW RIGHT ❈ A large clam shell and coral-colored table lamp nod to the coastal setting.

Cottage Revival

WHEN MY FAMILY and I left Atlanta in 2004 to open Tracery in Rosemary Beach we wanted to embrace the spirit of coastal living in our life and our home. And our idea of the quintessential beach house is a wood-framed cracker cottage.

Mark, Mallory, and I couldn't find anything that fit our needs and were considering building an old Florida classic from scratch when we learned the local Methodist church was selling its parsonage to make way for a fellowship hall. We are an environmentally responsible family and started exploring the options. Decades before green design was all the fashion, moving a house was an economical way to recoup the materials and labor invested in the original construction. Relocating and renovating an existing structure is one of the most efficient ways to reuse.

After purchasing the parsonage, we found a 110-by-130-foot wooded lot on a corner in the historic beach community of Seagrove. The neighborhood is famous for its old-growth oaks and magnolias, so we personally walked the property, marking big trees to preserve the mature native landscape. With all the permits in hand and new footings in place, moving the house was relatively easy thanks to Ducky Johnson House Movers, who have been relocating structures for more than fifty years.

The route was a straight shot about four miles along a county road with one major intersection. The movers cut the structure in half and loaded it. Once they got on the road, everything happened quickly. A pair of blue-lace curtains in the kitchen window were still hanging when the house was leveled into position on the new foundation.

OPPOSITE ❋ I'm constantly rearranging the furniture. A collection of antique trophies and native greenery from the garden are one of many ever-changing vignettes in my living room.

The basic arrangement of rooms was retained, but we made a few courageous changes to introduce volume, natural light, and architectural character. We stripped away the original eight-foot dropped ceiling in the living and dining area, exposing a series of trusses and rafters. Sixteen nautical glass pendants hang between the rafters to accentuate the volume of the peaked ceiling, and the structural members are painted a crisp shade of white for a loft-like feel.

The renovation highlights the traditional materials and vernacular details of the original structure and provides a historic reference for a more contemporary layering of my own personal style. It's home, that's for sure.

OPPOSITE ❈ New wide-plank horizontal paneling adds character, and a coat of white paint combined with uncovered HVAC ducts enhances the loft-like quality. A painting by Courtney Garrett hangs above the sofa.

ABOVE ❈ Stainless steel open shelving introduces a contemporary touch in the kitchen. Paintings, family portraits, and vintage collections animate nearly every surface.

RIGHT ❁ Shades of neutrals are limitless. Calming hues of grays, blues, and greens inform our master bedroom. New French doors swing open to connect with the screen porch.

OPPOSITE ❁ I love combining the unexpected and showing how different styles and periods can live happily side by side. And I'm always ready to take risks.

OPPOSITE ✼ The porch is so personal. A coat of fire-engine red paint updates the vintage glider, rocker, and side chairs, found by my mother at different times—one from a yard sale, one from a flea market, and one from a neighbor. The coffee table was made by my grandfather in his high school shop class.

LEFT ✼ The original scale and massing of the cottage establish an unassuming demeanor along the street in keeping with the character of the town of Seagrove.

Along the Waterfront

A home at the beach should be more than just another house.

It should set the stage for a different outlook on life.

Endless Vistas

SET HIGH ALONG a natural bluff, this vacation home overlooking the Gulf of Mexico engages its setting with enthusiasm, blending low-key sophistication and high-style waterfront living. Doors recede to embrace the pool terrace and panoramic views. Life moves effortlessly between indoors and outdoors.

Although the house had been completed only a few years earlier, original finishes were dark, heavy-handed, and dated before their time. However, the new owners, who had worked with Anna Kay Porch and me on another project, found much to like about the property. At first, they weren't sure they wanted to take on a renovation, but in the end the setting won out.

Their objective was pretty straightforward: a bright, airy, playful retreat for big family gatherings and summer vacations. We opted for fresh colors, new surfaces, and cosmetic changes rather than major structural modifications.

With twelve-foot ceilings and lofty windows along three walls, the main space begged for continuity while still giving credence to both the dining and conversation areas. Anna Kay and I started with a background of whites to lighten things throughout and then layered neutrals and differing degrees of color as you move through the house. We didn't want the draperies to compete with the view, so we used simple white with a wide gray border for all the first-floor windows.

OPPOSITE ❂ There's no more relaxing sound than the cadenced lapping of gentle waves along the beach. An infinity pool, lounge chairs, and something cool to drink make for a perfect afternoon.

ABOVE ⊗ In the living area, up-holstered pieces mix textures and patterns that were chosen for comfort and durability. Tall white linen draperies with a gray border act as parentheses to views out.

OPPOSITE ⊗ We chose complementary colors and finishes for the kitchen and dining area, with varying tones and detailing to give each space personality.

Two comfortable sofas and a generous jute rug anchor the living area. The palette nods to the more muted tones of nature—sand, shells, and driftwood. The dining table's prime location was sure to see double duty, so we chose host chairs that could be pulled into the living room. Washable slipcovers on the slipper chairs and a white faux leather on the bench are sturdy enough to withstand wet swimsuits.

Because the kitchen was in the center of the action, we updated the space with a working-counter dining island, a tile backsplash, limestone counters, and white cabinets all tailored for relaxed entertaining. A fully outfitted guest penthouse occupies the top floor. For continuity, we used similar finishes and colors, allowing the space to be a more integral part of the house while still offering a sense of retreat for guests and anyone who wants to take in the penthouse view.

An open plan reflects the way families gather at the beach. The dining table is positioned to encourage easy access to the pool terrace and great outdoors.

OPPOSITE ❈ The master suite is located on the second floor with its own private porch overlooking the Gulf. The bed nestles into a niche painted a deep shade of aquamarine.

LEFT ❈ A comfy armchair and ottoman anchor a sunny corner of the bedroom. Colors, art, and accessories defer to the waterfront setting.

ABOVE ❈ The top floor is a dedicated penthouse style guest suite outfitted with a kitchen, bar, and living area with four slipcovered chairs encircling a leather drum ottoman.

OPPOSITE ❈ You could never forget this house is right on the Gulf of Mexico, but it's still an unexpected treat every time you step through the expansive glass doors and onto the third-floor porch.

Texas Gulf-Coast Kaleidoscope

 THERE'S A LIGHTHEARTED spirit and inherent change in attitude that comes with the territory of designing a home by the sea. It's where you are not only allowed but encouraged to have some fun.

First, a house along the water is the place to embrace color both inside and out. Sure, a house painted a soft shade of aqua in Dallas or Houston might not work, but in the beach town of Cinnamon Shore along the Texas Gulf Coast, it's a perfect fit.

During the summer of 2009, the clients toured the *Southern Living* Idea House and loved everything about the design, all the colors, the town, and of course, the view. I was thrilled about doing another house along the same stretch of beach, and doubly excited since they had hired Mark as their architect. That was a nice bonus. With a fresh take on the familiar, Mark's architecture responds to the practicalities of vernacular design with inviting covered porches, deep overhangs, shading, shadows, and lots of windows.

The house is nestled behind a buffer of dunes and native plants, so Mark inverted the floor plan, allowing living spaces to take advantage of views and prevailing breezes. The kitchen anchors the heart of the grand, second-story space with a pair of symmetrical islands.

And then there's the color. Certain beach towns have their own trademark tones. Nantucket is known for navy and white; Palm Beach

OPPOSITE ❋ The aqua-and-white color combination makes for a bright and cheerful open kitchen. Casual meals and informal entertaining are the norm at the beach, so we placed two counter-dining islands end-to-end.

has pink and green. If the Gulf Coast has a signature combination, it's likely aqua and white.

The Gulf's definitive color becomes this space, with a backsplash of aqua glass tile and six bar stools slipcovered with a sturdy, washable cotton. The dining table takes a different color turn with equally practical white slipcovered chairs and aqua placemats and accessories.

In the living area, I chose super-comfy upholstered pieces and added a pop of coral to the mix. It's the perfect complement to aqua. For a twist in the master suite, I reversed the combination and used coral as the primary color with hints of aqua.

The most memorable houses offer a reassuring familiarity to draw people in. The eye-catching aqua exterior and graceful porches offer a hint of things to come inside the congenial interiors. It's fun and a true retreat for simply relaxing at the beach . . . the most pleasurable escape of all.

OPPOSITE ❋ Exposed beams and a steeply sloping ceiling inform the master suite with a shipshape sense of craftsmanship. With its perch on the third floor, the cozy seating area enjoys panoramic views.

ABOVE ❋ Large windows flood the master bath with natural light. Wide-plank wood floors, Shaker-style cabinets, and vertical paneling instill a friendly cottage feel.

OVERLEAF ❋ The living room revels in the immeasurable sights and sounds of the Gulf. The décor is all about the beach.

ABOVE ❈ The children's wing exudes an invitation to linger and relax. Four built-in double bunks and a pair of day beds accommodate lots of friends and family.

BELOW ❈ Painted horizontal paneling, clever storage, and pillow-topped benches make for a fun and functional bathroom configuration.

OPPOSITE ❈ In the first-floor guest suite, embroidered linens and whimsical nautical art make the most of the cool aqua color scheme.

RIGHT ❀ The rules are different at a house along the water. The front door opens into an utterly practical foyer outfitted with a long row of storage cubbies and hooks. The sand stops here.

OPPOSITE ❀ From the street, this Gulf-front house presents a reassuringly familiar stance with multiple porches, carpenter-detailed pillars and brackets, varied rooflines, and welcoming proportions.

Rosemary Revelries

 **NO MATTER** the style or size, a beach house should foster an easygoing atmosphere and evoke the spirit of the place. That's exactly the vibe we were trying to create for a young family who escape the hustle and bustle of Atlanta every chance they get. Whether for a weekend or longer, they head south to Rosemary Beach, a New Urbanist town founded more than twenty years ago along the Gulf of Mexico and named for the native plant that grows freely along the dunes.

Reflective of the town's British West Indies–inspired architecture, the home's exterior presented a pleasing mix of masonry and wood in earth tones to the street, but its interiors seriously needed updating. Everything about a second home suggests a casual approach, and we happily followed that lead in our top-to-bottom renovation. We played up the positives of the original structure, starting with views to the water and the gracious open living spaces on the third floor enlivened with rough-hewn cypress beams and a peaked wooden ceiling. Saluting the British colonial mix of complementary darks and lights, we outfitted a contemporary new kitchen with a mix of dark brown on the lower cabinets in the otherwise white kitchen. Ebony-stained French doors and floors throughout continue this aesthetic.

To retain a fun and casual mood, we opted for finishes and fabrics that withstand sandy feet and salty swimsuits. The dining table and

OPPOSITE ⊗ A brown and aqua chevron rug anchors the living area. Simple white draperies frame tall windows and doors that open onto a balcony with views to the Gulf. Plush pillows with nautical patterns make for a comfortable corner window seat.

sideboard are crafted of reclaimed teak with clean, simple lines. The white leather chairs and slipcovered host chairs are equal parts practical and posh.

In the living room, the sectional carves out a generous gathering spot for the whole family that includes a fireplace and a cozy built-in bench in the corner window. I wanted to give this space a splatter of coastal colors, and nothing says the Gulf like aqua in varied patterns and prints.

With sunlight flooding in and the French doors swung open, this weekend house exudes an invitation to unwind. It's the reason we all love to come to the beach.

OPPOSITE ❧ In the dining area, the atmosphere is informal and inviting. Dark wood floors, espresso lower cabinets, and rough-hewn cypress beams counter the otherwise white kitchen. The table and sideboard are crafted of reclaimed teak, the perfect family-friendly material.

ABOVE ❧ Throughout, the décor is simplified and restrained. An abstract landscape pairs with the clean lines of the modern farm table and contemporary silhouette of the white leather chairs.

Blues, browns, and soft linens define
the master bedroom. Matching side
tables and aqua lamps flank the
plush upholstered headboard.

The adjacent bath features a mix of contemporary lines and natural textures. The upper walls and ceilings are painted a pale aqua, complementing the darker surfaces. The flooring is a pebbled tile. The large beach painting balances the wood shelves on the opposite wall.

OPPOSITE ❈ Downstairs spaces transition from coastal casual to completely kid-friendly with the change of wall colors, whimsical accessories, and of course, toys. The rolling barn door creates an open exchange between the playroom and bedrooms.

LEFT ❈ Old maps mounted in shadowboxes and a vintage marble-topped chest create a focal point in the children's wing.

The option for guests to retreat to their own sanctuary is especially appealing at the beach. This carriage house is a deliberate departure from the overall aesthetic of the main house. Although the space is compact, we went for bolder colors and a single work of art over the sofa.

Amid the Dunes

 **A HOUSE ALONG** the water is a luxury to be embraced on every level. Simple cottages and grand compounds up and down every shore have long reflected the spirit of the place and possessed a lighthearted spirit all their own.

Overlooking expansive dunes and the Gulf of Mexico in WaterSound Beach, this home nods to the shingle-style traditions of the Northeast with the practicalities of Southern vernacular architecture. The house was recently completed but had never been fully furnished when clients looking to purchase it asked me to offer suggestions.

The place is amazing, and the structure had character. Rather than starting from scratch, we decided to embrace what was before us—most of all the view.

Like many contemporary beach houses, the main living spaces are located on the second floor. Without walls in this soaring grand hall of a room, it was up to us to place furniture to give definition to the various functions and take full advantage of vistas from every vantage point. The dining table dwells front and center at the top of the stairway. In a cozy conversation nook four identical chairs surround a custom white-leather ottoman, while the main living area focuses on a large fireplace. Both groupings encourage easy exchange with the large Gulf-side porch. It's all about creating areas to gather and spend time together.

The existing horizontal wood planking on the walls, the dark wood flooring, and distinctive basket-weave ceiling create an envelope of robust finishes, so I countered with softer neutrals and bold colors in the

OPPOSITE ❈ Retreating to the coast is about being in touch with nature and relaxation. This deep covered porch off the second-floor living room is the perfect spot to do just that.

In a sunny corner of the living room, four oversize chairs slipcovered in a casual cotton-linen blend circle a drum-style ottoman. Its faux leather and nail-head trim are designed to withstand sandy feet.

art and furnishings. Shades of aquamarine and lime green made total sense in a waterfront setting, so I paired patterned fabrics with a mix of solids starting in the living room and continuing throughout. A series of screened breezeways, breaking up the scale and massing of the house, connects several guest bedrooms, making each one feel like a retreat all its own.

Equally as engaging as the gracious interiors are the porches, each with its own distinctive personality. Whether you're sunning on the third-floor balcony or napping on a shaded side porch, this is a house to savor the joys of coastal living.

The emotional appeal of aquamarine blues and emerald greens are the perfect inflection for a beach house. Inside and out, we used colors that ignite the senses while offering a sense of calm and cool.

Nearly every room turns onto the view. The diagonal wall directs the bed toward a bay window. The trim was already painted this bold shade of aquamarine. I found the perfect fabric for the draperies and the rest of the room followed suit. The geometric pillows and bed linens pick up the burnt orange of the floral print.

ABOVE ❈ The built-in bed and continuous bank of windows create the illusion of a sleeping porch that might have been filled in over time.

OPPOSITE ❈ An open terrace off the third-floor master bedroom offers commanding views of WaterSound's expansive coastal landscape.

In Harmony

Architecture and interiors should go hand in hand,

yet different styles, periods, and approaches can live happily side by side.

We Belong to the Land

CARLTON LANDING is a New Urbanist town along Lake Eufaula in Oklahoma. When town founders Grant and Jen Humphreys came to us to design their home, we were honored. Carlton Landing already boasted an impressive design team starting with town planners Andrés Duany and Elizabeth Plater-Zybert, who had also designed Seaside, Rosemary Beach, and Alys Beach along Scenic 30A.

Building one of the first houses in Carlton Landing, Grant and Jen understood that both the exterior and interior would set the stage for the emerging community. They had already tapped architect Kenny Craft to design their home. They wanted an interior designer who understood their vision and appreciated the spirit of this place, and on a more practical level, Grant and Jen needed a comfortable home where they could raise their five children (Emma, Ford, Jack, Mary, and Hank), two chocolate labs (Bud and Dixie), and several backyard chickens.

The heart of any home—especially one in the heartland of America—is the kitchen. The Humphreys family gathers around the dining table every night with each of the children recapping highlights of the day. The large island offers plenty of space to spread out for homework while Jen prepares dinner, often with eggs from their chicken coop and vegetables from their garden. It also serves as a working kitchen for visiting chefs who come to teach culinary classes in Carlton Landing.

OPPOSITE ❋ The home offers inherent flexibility in its architecture and furnishings. The den can be closed off for music lessons and doubles as a guest bedroom. The art is a family effort made from leftover construction lumber and chalkboard paint. Grant freehand scripted the verse.

OPPOSITE ⌘ Horizontal planks with wide spacing enliven the stairway and creates a strong backdrop for a painting by an Oklahoma artist. The red chest offer functional storage and dramatic focal point.

LEFT ⌘ The side door gets a lot of traffic from guests as well as the family. The simple black bench is the perfect staging area for coming and going. The sheer grace and utter charm of this family is a large part of this home's appeal.

OVERLEAF ⌘ The kitchen is front and center in the one large living space so we used a strong symmetrical arrangement, balancing the large communal space.

ABOVE ❈ Rather than individual bedrooms, the children have sleeping quarters. The three boys share a communal play area, while each has an alcove outfitted with a full bed, bookshelves, and storage.

OPPOSITE ❈ An active family of seven accumulates lots of stuff. A mudroom adjacent to the kitchen provides a designated basket and hook for each of the five children.

A cohesive flow of colors, textures, and materials runs throughout the home. There's no hierarchy of spaces and every room is inviting to family and friends. Neighborhood children stopping by on foot or bikes are just as likely to enter the front door that opens directly into the main living area, as they are the side door.

The side entry is truly a double-duty foyer, with a painting by Denise Duong, an Oklahoma artist, hung on axis. Keeping everything in perspective to the right of the door is an ever-changing collection of children's art and folk pieces above a simple black bench with five pairs of cowboy boots always ready to giddy-up and go.

The overriding spirit is welcoming and embracing, from the friends' foyer to the always-open kitchen to the kids' bunk rooms. This Oklahoma home is more than just OK.

OPPOSITE ❈ The simple and straightforward farmhouse stands tall and proud along Carlton Landing's main boulevard.

ABOVE ❈ The familiar form and inviting scale of the Carlton Landing schoolhouse recall simpler times.

LEFT ❈ Sunset view of Lake Eufaula from a community park.

No Place Like Home

 MOVING WASN'T REALLY an option. The clients adored the neighborhood, the street, and their home. It was a 1920s Tudor cottage that was extremely long on charm but awfully short on square footage. With four young children, it just wasn't big enough.

I had worked with the family on their lake house, so I had a good understanding of what they were looking for in their permanent residence. However, this was an ambitious renovation on a relatively small lot in a desirable Birmingham neighborhood, and I was happy to team up with Jeff Dungan of Dungan Nequette Architects.

The family moved into a rental practically next door, and construction began. The most dramatic change was relocating the original stairway from the foyer to the back of the house. This created a new family wing with a den, expanded kitchen, breakfast room, and master suite. Upstairs is devoted to the four children's bedrooms, so it seemed right to treat the stairway as a more private passageway rather than an exalted architectural statement.

The new arrangement is much better suited to the way an active young family lives today, and we were still able to keep the personality and quirks of the original house. The owners wanted white as the prevailing wall color, so I gave the floors a dark stain for high contrast. For a

OPPOSITE ❀ French antiques and refined vignettes set a tone of understated elegance. When working with a white palette, I study the combination of layers and textures until the balance feels right.

touch of drama in the foyer, I opted for an inlaid wooden pattern in the floor rather than a rug.

The house had a classic living and dining room, but they were not grand by any means. In keeping with the original scale of these elegant and intimate entertaining spaces, I selected upholstered furniture with crisp silhouettes and low backs. I paired these new pieces with a few pretty French antiques, all focused on the limestone fireplace. New paneling and a patterned detail on the ceiling add a thoughtful layering of tension and restraint.

There's definitely a hierarchy of formal and family spaces, but with a thread of easy elegance and sense of discovery. The house is more simply responsive than strictly classical. I like to think it's refined and relaxing and, in the end, timeless.

OPPOSITE ❋ In the living room, we deferred to the original architecture. The fireplace is the natural resting point, but we reinforced the formality with wall paneling and a patterned ceiling. Silk and velvet striped pillows add moments of color.

ABOVE ❋ A framed vintage wallpaper fragment mounted above an antique French chest in the foyer is a fitting introduction of things to come.

ABOVE ❈ The office nook repeats the same color as the cabinets in the adjacent kitchen. I try to avoid deliberately overcomplicating things. A series of traditional silhouettes lines the wall.

RIGHT ❈ Large-scale patterned wallpaper and distressed mirrored tiles impart drama in a small powder room.

OPPOSITE ❈ Whenever appropriate I honored the good bones and unique character of the original house. The new breakfast room establishes long views and fosters a gracious exchange between old and new.

The kitchen was reconfigured to be open and accessible for a young family, but timeless in spirit. The wood ceiling adds warmth and the industrial-style pendant lights are simple and sculptural. One-by-two-inch marble bricks define the backsplash, which runs to the ceiling. The custom range hood was crafted by a local metalworker, who used car paint and layered stainless steel strapping.

RIGHT ❈ The expanded family wing includes a den wrapped in paint-glazed pecky cypress paneling. The new stairway links family spaces with the children's four bedrooms on the second floor.

OPPOSITE ❈ The den's new marble fireplace is substantial but not overly ornate. The pecky cypress instills depth and character to built-in bookcases.

OPPOSITE ❁ A new master wing on the first floor is a soothing and private oasis. The palette is predominately whites and grays with layers of texture adding visual interest.

LEFT ❁ The antique claw-foot tub was original to the house. It was salvaged and refinished to complement new fixtures and the marble walls and floors.

Music City Medley

AUTHENTIC MATERIALS and handcrafted details compose a gracious marriage between elegance and unpretentiousness in this rambling family home in Nashville. From every vantage point, the house is an orchestrated sequence that gradually unfolds to reveal equal measure of sophistication and down-home comfort. Details are considered and honed for a look and feel that is natural, seamless, and welcoming.

Construction had just started on the house when the owners came to me. Architect Blaine Bonadies had composed a series of interconnected wings that turn inward to a garden courtyard and open outward to engage the Tennessee landscape. It was going to be a wonderful home, and I was excited about the possibilities.

The client has a great appreciation and understanding of design and wanted to work with an interior designer who shared her aesthetic and could relate to the family's relaxed lifestyle. She had dozens of Pinterest boards with thousands of photographs, and it turned out most of her pins were of Tracery's work. We set up a meeting, and from there everything clicked, and the design came together like the best of any artistic collaboration. We love working with clients who are engaged while giving us freedom to roam creatively.

Although the house encompasses approximately 8,500 square feet, the free-flowing arrangement of rooms with one opening into the next

creates an easygoing spirit. The deft handling of materials and craftsman-ship reflects the handiwork of artisan builder Brady Fry, while the home's natural setting is enhanced by the talents of landscape architect Anne Daigh. Even in the most formal spaces, from the massive stone fireplace and grand piano in the living room to the bold splashes of green against a wall of graphic black and white in the dining room, the home is utterly contented and comfortable.

Inside and out, the house is less about issues of style than appropri-ateness. The kitchen is the absolute center of this family-friendly home. It's sunny, cheerful, and bright, and always active.

The house finished up last year, but my relationship with the family is ongoing. We are currently working on a guest house and music studio, and we came back at Christmas to help decorate for the holidays. We've even flown up for a weekend to attend a concert. No matter if we are working on plans for the next project or just relaxing, we tend to gather around the kitchen island. It's the rhythm and soul of this Tennessee home.

Even the most formal rooms are fam-ily spaces. Everyone gathers around the massive stone fireplace in the liv-ing room on winter nights, and piano practice is conducted on the grand piano. As soon as I saw the antique clock, I knew it would be perfect for the space in terms of its scale and playful spirit. Sometimes an object becomes a work of art.

The kitchen is fundamentally sparse in its colors relative to the rest of the house, yet it comes alive with multiple layers of materials, textures, finishes, and tons of natural light. The large island provides space for family meals and casual entertaining. Custom-designed benches and bar stools are clustered around one end. Subway tile with dark grout wraps the kitchen and rises to the ceiling.

OPPOSITE ❈ If the interplay of styles and color is the melody of this home, the movement throughout is the rhythm. The family room serves as a transition between private family wings and the formal dining room.

ABOVE ❈ Particular attention is paid to halls and stairs. Two guest suites are accessed by a second stairway for privacy from the children's wing. Family photographs animate the landing.

BELOW ❈ In the freestanding pool house, an eclectic mix of contemporary and casual furniture, selective pops of bold colors, and whimsical art reflects the family's carefree spirit.

OVERLEAF ❈ A contemporary home designed for a relaxed lifestyle and crafted with venerable materials is exactly what the family wanted. It's a joy to collaborate with talented professionals on a project executed with such attention to detail.

ABOVE ✦ A sculptural, pour-in-place concrete seating area and fire pit anchor a sheltered corner of the pool terrace.

BELOW ✦ The home wraps around a central courtyard. Hanging carnival lights and facing sofas make for an inviting space for entertaining.

OPPOSITE LEFT ✦ Firmly grounded, the structure cuts a memorable profile against the Tennessee sky.

OPPOSITE RIGHT ✦ The gray striped diagonal paneling and a chevron ceiling create a dramatic first impression in the formal entry.

OPPOSITE ❋ The studio office is paneled and dark, but a million miles from a typical cloistered library space. A full-size vintage motorcycle hanging from the ceiling and fire-engine red velour chairs say it all.

THIS PAGE ❋ A contemporary stairway connects the master suite with the children's upstairs wing, where their own paintings are artfully displayed. A new house is a blank canvas waiting to be drawn upon. I always encourage the family to make their mark.

OPPOSITE ❋ The master suite accommodates his and hers closets. Hers is a showcase of high fashion and personal style.

LEFT ❋ A medley of taupes, grays, and hints of gold soothes the senses in the master bedroom. A well-designed home should reflect the personality, sincerity, and passions of the people who live there.

OVERLEAF LEFT ❋ The guest wing features two guest suites, each with steeply sloping ceilings. Geometrical patterns in the rug and curtains enliven the restful gray color scheme.

OVERLEAF RIGHT ❋ I treat a bathroom like any other important space in a home, embellishing it with textures, rich materials, fabrics, and accessories. Think of the tub as a piece of furniture, in terms of the lines, the scale in relationship to the room, and of course, comfort.

Acknowledgments

First and foremost, I am thankful for the opportunity to be a designer. I love my job. I love to create homes for my clients, and now I get to share some of those homes with all of you.

Without my family I would not be where I am today: Mark is my constant companion, fellow traveler, designer, and husband. Mallory is my daughter and a college student pursuing her dreams. She is creative, loves life, loves people, and will explore the world. Dad and my stepmom, Anne, are always there for me and have encouraged me personally and in my business; they are the parents that I can always call for guidance in all parts of my life. They are a treasure. Mom is my rock; she is a constant in my life and in the lives of my family members. She is beautiful inside and out, and I am so happy she is my mother. My sisters Megan and Maggie understand everything about me. Sisters are the greatest gift.

My clients are amazing people, and I have loved getting to know every one of them. First, I thank them for inviting us to design their homes. And my thanks to all those who opened their homes to us for this book. Thanks for letting our photographers, stylist, and the Tracery team into your home to document it.

The team at Tracery is extra special. This book would not have been possible without them: Thank you to Anna Kay Porch, my lead designer and constant sidekick for the last nine years. She is my other half at work, and knows what I am going to say even before I do. Anna Kay started as an intern at Tracery and has become a confident and extremely capable interior designer. Her talent is apparent every day. Heather Day, my bookkeeper and the person behind the scenes of Tracery, has worked with me for almost ten years. She knows everything about Tracery and keeps us moving forward. I want to thank her for all of her years of work and the many more to come. Thank you, Leslie Cristina, for managing the Tracery shop and being the ever-smiling face for our visitors in Rosemary Beach. Jenny Dargavell, our "queen of randomness," has a different job every day at Tracery and does it all with a smile. Beth Nash is new to the design team and the Tracery family. Thank you to Michaela, Mom, and Mallory for watching the shop, visiting with our customers, and adding something a little special to their homes. Over the years there have been many others helping us make Tracery what it is today, and I thank them for their contributions. In particular, I want to thank those who contributed to the work seen in this book: Jan, Bess, Doug, and Kristina.

I will be forever grateful to Jeff Dungan and Louis Nequette for the opportunity they gave me more than ten years ago to follow my dreams, move to the beach with my family, and design beautiful homes. I can't thank them enough for changing the course of my life. I look forward to designing more beautiful places together in the future. This is only the beginning.

While attending the Auburn University School of Architecture, a few professors greatly influenced my design career. Thank you to Magdelena Garmaz, Gaines Blackwell, Rusty Smith, Andy Goldsborough, and David Braly. At ASD in Atlanta, where I began my career, I am forever thankful to Michael Neiswander, Steve Yancey, and Thom Williams.

My deepest appreciation goes to Abrams for giving me the opportunity to make this book. It has been a pleasure working first with editor Dervla Kelly then with editor Andrea Danese, managing editor Michael Clark, and associate art director Darilyn Carnes.

Other people I want to thank: Jean Allsopp, Frank Craige, Kristen Payne, Lindsay Bierman, Doretta Sperduto, Tom Adams, Jennifer Green, Mary Ann Whitehall, Jeff Lamkin, Erin Oden, Larry Davis, Dixie McCurley, Lucy Fry, Sheila Goode, Wayne and Maureen Schnell, Erin Pfister, Krissi Finch, Carol Murphy Rauschkolb, Mary Lee Wyatt, Savanna Guess, Sarah Green, Cheryl Graves, Peggy Williams, and Kevin Boyle.

And last but not least, thank you to a colleague and one of my best friends, Lynn Nesmith. From that first day on the beach when she suggested that we create a book about Tracery, it has been a fun and wonderful journey. Lynn and I have had many tiring days of travel, photo shoots, writing, reviewing, and editing, but we had a great time doing it. This is Lynn's fifth book, and I am grateful she is the one telling the stories of my designs. She understands my voice and told the stories beautifully. Cheers to you, Lynn, and the many sunsets to come!

Credits

Tudor Renaissance, Birmingham, Alabama
Architect: Jeff Dungan, Dungan Nequette Architects, dungan-nequette.com
Landscape Designer: Norman Kent Johnson
Photographer: Jean Allsopp, jeanallsopp.com

Lofty Lakeside Living, Lake Martin, Alabama
Builder: John Lanier
Photographer: Jean Allsopp

Steeped in Tradition, Florida
Original Architect: Martin-Hosmer Studios
Photographer: Jean Allsopp

Fashion Starts at Home, Seagrove, Florida
Photographer: Jean Allsopp

Altitude Adjustment, Aspen, Colorado
Architect: Whipple and Brewster, whippleandbrewster.com
Local Design Consultant: Melissa Glenn
Photographer: Brent Moss, brentmossphoto.com

Small-Town Values, *Southern Living* Idea House, Senoia, Georgia
Architect: Historical Concepts, historicalconcepts.com
Developer: Scott Tigchelaar, The Historic Senoia Project, historicsenoia.com
Photographer: Laurey W. Glenn, courtesy of *Southern Living* Magazine

Sheltered Existence, Seagrove, Florida
Photographer: Jean Allsopp

Sweet Home Alabama, Kinston, Alabama
Architect: Gaines Blackwell, Auburn, Alabama
Design Consultant: Louise Wright
Photographer: Jean Allsopp

Good Neighbors, Rosemary Beach, Florida
Architect: Peter Block, peterblockarchitects.com

Builder: Chad Christenson, Kenson Group
Town Plan: Duany Plater-Zyberk & Company, dpz.com
Community: Rosemary Beach, rosemarybeach.com
Photographer: Laura Resen, courtesy of *Veranda* Magazine, lauraresen.com

The Spice of Life, *Southern Living* Idea House, Port Aransas, Texas
Architect: Louis Nequette, Dungan Nequette Architects
Developer: Jeff Lamkin, Sea Oats Group, Inc., seaoatsgroup.com
Landscape Design: Buffel Grass Seed Co., buffelgrassseed.com
Builder: Keystone Builders, keystonepa.com
Town Plan: Mark Schnell, Schnell Urban Design, schnellurbandesign.com
Community: Cinnamon Shore, cinnamonshore.com
Photographer: Laurey W. Glenn, courtesy of *Southern Living* Magazine

Alys Beach Escape, Alys Beach, Florida
Architect: Eric Watson, ericwatson.com
Courtyard Landscape Architect: Khoury-Vogt Architects
Town Plan: Duany Plater-Zyberk & Company
Community: Alys Beach, alysbeach.com
Photographer: Jean Allsopp

Cottage Revival, Seagrove, Florida
Photographer: Jean Allsopp

Endless Vistas, Seagrove, Florida
Architect: Russell Johnson
Photographer: Jean Allsopp

Texas Gulf-Coast Kaleidoscope, Port Aransas, Texas
Architect: Mark Schnell, Schnell Urban Design, schnellurbandesign.com
Photographer: Jean Allsopp

Rosemary Revelries, Rosemary Beach, Florida
Architect: Eric Watson
Photographer: Jean Allsopp

Amid the Dunes, WaterSound Beach, Florida
Architect: Kenneth Lynch, Kenneth Lynch & Associates, kennethlynch.com
Builder: Mark Breaux, Breaux Construction
Photographer: Jean Allsopp

We Belong to the Land, Carlton Landing, Oklahoma
Architect: Kenny Craft, craftdesign-studio.com
Exterior Elevations Architect: Steve Mouzon, Mouzon Design, mouzon.com
Builder: Traditional Craft Homes, LLC
Town Plan: Duany Plater-Zybert & Company
Town Founders: Grant and Jen Humphreys
Community: Carlton Landing, carltonlanding.com
Photographer: Jean Allsopp

No Place Like Home, Birmingham, Alabama
Architect: Jeff Dungan, Dungan Nequette Architects
Photographer: Jonny Valiant, jonnyvaliant.com

Music City Medley, Nashville, Tennessee
Architect: Blaine Bonadies, bonadiesarchitect.com
Landscape Architect: Anne Daigh, annedaigh.com
Builder: Brady Fry, fryclassicconstruction.com
Photographer: Jean Allsopp

Overleaf: An ornate framed painting hangs against an antique glass-mirrored walls in a historic Tudor home.

Editor: Andrea Danese
Designer: Darilyn Lowe Carnes
Production Manager: Denise LaCongo

Library of Congress Control Number: 2014942994

ISBN: 978-1-61769-155-3

Text copyright © 2015 Eleanor Lynn Nesmith
Photographs copyright © 2015 Jean Allsopp

Printed and bound in China
10 9 8 7 6 5 4 3 2 1

Stewart, Tabori & Chang books are available at special discounts when purchased in quantity for premiums and promotions as well as fundraising or educational use. Special editions can also be created to specification. For details, contact specialsales@abramsbooks.com or the address below.

THE ART OF BOOKS SINCE 1949
115 West 18th Street
New York, NY 10011
www.abramsbooks.com